# Where Do I Start?

## HINTS and TIPS
### for
## BEGINNING GENEALOGISTS
### with
## ONLINE RESOURCES
#### by

### Donna Causey

12/1/2012

Best Wishes Sheri!

Donna R. Causey

**DEDICATION**
This book is dedicated to my wonderful
family with thanks for understanding
my obsession with
history, writing and genealogy

# My Initiation into the Fascinating World of Genealogy

When I was young, my family often attended family reunions and I loved hearing the stories passed down from one generation to the next, but genealogy research never had much appeal. It seemed like a considerable amount of time was spent collecting names of ancestors and how they were related. Name collecting did not interest me; I enjoyed the stories more.

Then I attended a family reunion with my mother after I retired. Our family historian, Hal Cottingham, shared stories and anecdotes about some of our ancestors at the reunion and I became fascinated. I wanted to learn more so I visited with him a few days later. Hal pulled out a box of records, letters and documents about our family which he and my deceased gr-uncle accumulated over many years. I was amazed at their work and asked if I could make copies, organize and protect the documents from deterioration. He readily agreed and I took the box home.

As I looked through over 200 years of data, I was amazed. My gr-uncle Daniel Snead Cottingham searched for and found the first place our ancestor's resided in Bibb County, Alabama in the early 1800's. Any remnants of their home was gone but he discovered the small cemetery nearby, with tombstones of our first Cottingham ancestors in Alabama. The cemetery was in the middle of forest land on private property, off a dirt road, and completely overgrown. I don't know how he managed to find it. Family members attacked the overgrowth and slowly recovered the cemetery. A sign was placed at it's entrance and my cousin's family continues to maintain the cemetery.

My gr-uncle, my mother and cousin communicated with other relatives and connected our family to Cottingham's in North and South Carolina. They completed all this research without the aid of computer. Again, I was astonished at their endeavor.

In Hal's records, I found a book by Ana Cottingham of Oklahoma, compiled on the Cottingham's of Alabama. Ana extended our family research west into Arkansas, Louisiana, Mississippi, Oklahoma and Texas. My mother and Hal Cottingham were also in touch with, John Cottingham, a family historian in North Carolina. John was a certified genealogist and he discovered the first Cottingham immigrant who arrived in on the Eastern Shore of Virginia around the early 1600's. He made a trip to England where he verified that our Cottingham family came from Cottingham, England.

I continued working with the records and I felt compelled to visit the place my ancestor's arrived in America. On our next vacation, my husband and I visited the Eastern Shore and found the location of the Cottingham's plantation. Standing on the land and looking toward Plantation Creek, I realized that I was looking at the same scene my ancestor, Thomas Cottingham, and his wife Mary viewed everyday. This realization filled me with a overwhelming emotion and strong connection to my ancestry. At that moment, I guess you could say I was 'bitten by the genealogy bug' and never looked back.

Throughout my genealogical journey, I have been helped by numerous researchers and genealogists and thanks to their suggestions, my research has been much easier. I continued to expand my family tree and by 2007, I had over 40,000 people on my computer related to each other. In the world of genealogy, there is a sharing and caring community and I came to a decision in 2007 to share my research with others so I launched a website www.alabamapioneers.com.

While I gathered facts and data, I often wondered why my ancestors left their homes and moved to totally unknown locales. This required research into historical events at each location to uncover their motives. The trip to the Eastern Shore where my direct ancestor, Mary (Willson) Pattenden (of the Cottingham family) first settled in America became the catalyst for me to write my first historical fiction novel, *Ribbon of Love.* I continued searching  court documents, history books, and visited England for clues. I discovered information not typically found in American history books. Gradually, Mary's fictionalized life story evolved and *Ribbon of Love* was born. I am continuing the Cottingham's story  in my historical fiction series, *Tapestry of Love. Ribbon of Love* was published in 2011 and *Faith and Courage,* 2nd in the series will be published in the summer of 2012.

Through my website www.alabamapioneers.com, I receive emails from beginning family researchers with questions on how and where to begin. This book has been written to answer some of those questions. It is my hope, that it will alleviate a few of the difficulties a new researcher faces and become a guide so you may one day experience the joy I felt when I stood on the same land where my ancestor's trod so many years ago. Who knows?

You might be inspired to write your own novel/novels about your family.

## Tip Number One
## INVEST IN A COMPUTER

Of course, family historians and genealogists can research their family trees without a computer, but the benefits of a computer far out weigh the cost. Sitting at my desk in the morning with a cup of coffee and my feet propped up recording data is my ideal way to add to my family tree. A computer saves many hours of time and with the aid of family tree software, data, photographs, and documents can be recorded and easily organized. Most family tree software programs today are simple to use and very intuitive. Even if you do not have computer skills now, you can often find classes for learning how to use a computer at local libraries. Some are even free.

Laptop computers are especially valuable. They become a portable tool on research trips. With a laptop computer, information can be typed directly into the computer, saving quite a bit of time and you'll be able to quickly print out data for your surname file. The computer need not be expensive to be efficient but be sure the family tree software program you use enables you to do the following:

1) Record individual data easily. ( In most programs today, you only have to type an individual's data in one time.)
2) Allow for notes, documents, photographs, and etc. to be included with the individual data.
3) Connects individuals together. (some will do this automatically and even suggest connections.)

5

4) Allows you to share and receive information with other researchers through a GEDCOM database program.
5) Prints out reports such as family group sheets, charts, forms, etc.

An added advantage of a computer is the access to records all over the world through the internet and contacts you can make with other genealogy researchers, via emails and forums.

Many software programs today also allow you to add video clips, search databases automatically, and create family books and family trees.

Check Cindi's list for up to date information about software and computers. You can find Cindi's list at this website: http://www.cyndislist.com/software.htm

## Tip Number Two
# COLLECT YOUR DATA

## Ten Beginning Steps:
1) ALWAYS START WITH YOURSELF. This is the first thing any genealogist will tell you. Whether you use a computer or not, when you acquire documents about your family, it is often tempting to record the oldest ancestor's data first and move forward but this would be a mistake. You may find a gap and be unable to make the connection from you to this ancestor. There could also be errors in the data collected by others along the way. It is much safer to move backward in time than forward.

2) RECORD DATA ABOUT YOUR IMMEDIATE FAMILY Many times it is easy to skip this step in as you are enjoying the pursuit of a fruitful lead but soon you will be overwhelmed with scattered notes and papers. The papers have a way of disappearing over time and the effort you made will have been in vain. Remember, you are also recording data for future generations of family historians and they will appreciate the time you took to accurately record the data about your family.

3) CONTACT YOUR ELDERLY RELATIVES FOR FAMILY INFORMATION. Ask your grandparents, aunts uncles for information and offer to share your results. They may be in possession of a family member's prior research or completed some research themselves. Be sure to make reasonable requests and keep a copy of your any requests you made to avoid duplication. The copies will also provide

you with a list of future contacts. Always thank each person for their help.

4) SEARCH YOUR OWN HOUSE - You may already be in possession of information to record. Old photographs, heirlooms, family albums, old papers, newspaper clippings, diaries, letters, scrapbooks, Bibles, inscribed books, certificates, day planners, jewelry, resumes, report cards, handmade items, and yearbooks may provide insights into family history.

5) WRITE DOWN WHAT YOU REMEMBER - Explore and write down information from your own memory as far back as you can go in your family. You can document these memories later, just record them as notes in the beginning.

6) OTHER FAMILY MEMBER'S MEMORIES - Ask other members of your immediate family questions about what they remember and/or if they have any scrapbooks, newspapers clippings, diaries, Bibles, etc., they would be willing to share with you. Perhaps another family member is also working on the family tree. Offer to collaborate and share your results.

7) MAKE A LIST OF ALL ELDERLY MEMBERS. - After you make a list of all the elder members of the family, make plans to interview them soon. They will probably have a wealth of information to share. *

8) ATTEND FAMILY REUNIONS - Most families love to reminiscence at family reunions and many of your relatives will be in the mood to share their stories. Bring a recorder of some type to record the family stories but be sure to ask permission before recording anyone. Take careful written notes and include the date and source in all notes. Take photographs of everyone at the reunion and label the photographs. Try using the video part of your cell phone or

digital camera to record a video of your elderly relative telling the story. Future generations will appreciate it.

9) CEMETERIES - Visit the cemeteries of your family members, take photographs of tombstones and record the inscriptions, locations and any other data available. Be sure to take photographs of other related family members. Their tombstones may provide important clues if you ever hit a brickwall.

10) OLD HOME-PLACES - Visit old home-places or localities whenever possible, take photographs, and try to discover a little about the history of the area while visiting.

* See Sample Interview Questions in the Appendix at the end of this book for ideas of how to jog memories of elderly relatives.

## Tip Number Three
## ORGANIZE AND RECORD
## YOUR DATA

If you are successful in acquiring information, you will quickly become overwhelmed by all the paper clutter. This is when your computer becomes vital in your research. It will help you eliminate many papers and keep all your hard work easily accessible and organized.

A scanner, digital camera or cell phone with a camera will be a great asset in dealing with paper clutter. You will be able to make copies of your documents and photographs and retain them on your computer or a labeled CD/DVD. There are now even websites available for storage and some are even free.

→ PROOF RECORDS - Genealogy data falls into different categories. The most valuable data is Proof records. These are the original death or birth certificates, marriage licenses, photographs and copies of correspondence from relatives and are sometimes called Primary sources. They are usually costly and need to be preserved. By making a scan of these documents and saving them to a backup file or CD/DVD, you are will ensure their safety and you'll be able to share them with others via the CD/DVD or computer file. If you make a habit of immediately scanning/copying each document you acquire, then save it on your computer in a file or CD/DVD before storing it safely, you will never regret it. Use good preservation methods for old documents and photos and handle them with care. Acid-free paper should be used on all Proof documents and keep them in a clean, dry, cool place. They should always remain at home. If the information on a document is needed for a genealogy trip, make a copy to take.

→ SECONDARY RESEARCH NOTES – Documents, correspondence and other information can be arranged by surname and places in file folders or binders. Other items in the Surname files could be a time line, family group sheet, research record, copies of primary documents and ancestor charts. This file/binder can be transported easily to locations where you are doing research.

→ SCANNING AND COPYING - If you develop a habit of scanning and/or copying all your documents, notes, correspondence, etc. from your surname file to your computer, you will automatically have a backup system for your data at the same time. Digital Cameras and Cell phone cameras often make good photographs of documents and can be used as an alternative for scanning.

→ SOFTWARE - Modern family tree software programs provide ways to link all the documents to individuals within your family tree, such as photos, census records, correspondence, certificates etc. Take the time to attach the records after each research trip and you will have it ready to print out for your secondary surname file/binder before your next research trip.

## Tip Number Four
# DOCUMENTATION

You have recorded and organized all you know and all your family memories, now it is important to document what you have learned.

- FAMILY GROUP SHEET - At this point in your research, you should have a FAMILY GROUP SHEET on each person in your family. There should be a sheet for yourself, your children, your parents, grandparents, aunts, uncles, cousins and as many people on who you are able to acquire information. Family group sheets are simply, research logs on a person. Genealogy software programs will print out sheets for you on each person. The sheets should be placed in the surname folder/binder so they can be easily transported to any search location.
- SOURCES - Always include the source of your information on the FAMILY GROUP SHEET. Source information is invaluable if you want to share your data or decide to publish a book about your family.
- DOCUMENTATION - There are many ways to document your research information. The best source is the people you have listed in on family group sheets. Bibles, Baby Books, funeral cards, school or employment awards, yearbooks, military records, journals, photographs, employment records, newspaper clippings or any other similar records supporting the

information you acquired are considered documentation. Ask your family members if they will allow you to make a copy or send you a copy of the record. If you have a cell phone with a camera handy, you can quickly take a digital photograph.

Below are some good sources often used to document family research.

→ PHOTOGRAPHS - As you look at the old photographs of your family members, be sure to check the back. Sometimes, important information may be recorded there. Of course, be tactful when requesting this information. Many people are very cautious about sharing personal information so do not despair if they resist, there are other ways to acquire proof through public resources. Try using your digital camera or cell phone camera to make a copy of the photograph. It takes a steady hand but many people have often acquired decent digital photographs of valuable documents or photographs.

→ CEMETERIES - Visit Cemeteries where your ancestor's are buried and record all the information you find on their tombstones. Other family members are usually buried close by so be sure to take the information on their tombstones as well. Take photographs of the tombstones whenever possible and include the GPS location of the cemetery with the photographs. Your descendants will appreciate this valuable information. Many old cemeteries and tombstones have disappeared over time and your photograph may be all that descendants have to record the death. Some great hints about taking good photographs of tombstones can be found at the website: http://genealogyhelpandhints.com. Share your cemetery photographs on the free website: findagrave.com and other researchers will benefit from your effort and you will have a safe place for future generations. You might also connect with a cousin through the website.

→ BIRTH CERTIFICATES - Obtain birth certificates on as many individuals in your group sheets as possible. Birth certificates often provide a wealth of information such as where the parents were at the time of the birth, their occupations, age and the mother's maiden name.

→ DEATH CERTIFICATES - Request copies of death certificates whenever possible. Often you will learn the, parents, place of the individuals birth, where the decease resided at the time of death, birth dates, cause of death and who reported the death.

→ OBITUARIES - After acquiring the death certificate and determining the residence at the time of a death, you may be able to find an obituary notice in the local newspaper archives. Long obituaries were written in the past with a wealth of information about other family members and friends. Many local libraries, or State Archives have old newspapers available for research and some are on microfiche, available for inter-library loan. Be aware, some data may be inaccurate depending on the person writing the obituary.

→ SOCIAL SECURITY RECORDS - Acquire Social Security records on deceased parents, and grandparents. There is usually quite a bit of data such as residence, birth-dates and correct spelling of names on Social Security records.

→ CHURCH MEMBERSHIP - Seek church records on the individuals included in your ancestry such as Baptism, Christening, Church Membership, Church Minutes, Marriages, Births, and deaths. Many churches kept extensive records on families in their church. The internet will become a great resource. Many records and actual documents are now being digitized by libraries, genealogical research centers and even individuals. It still takes time to research these records but it saves you from traveling great distances.

→ CLUB and ORGANIZATION MEMBERSHIPS - Be sure to check for Clubs or organizations in which your ancestor may have participated. Clubs and organizations were very popular before Television and Radio was invented. They provided a means for social connections. Sometimes, biographies and/or photographs can be obtained.

## Tip Number Five
# RESEARCHING
# CENSUS RECORDS

One of the most helpful assets in your research will be Census Records. Most governments count their population every ten years and especially in the United States, and many questions were asked in past censuses.

Today actual digitized photographs of census records are now available on the internet. The 1940 census was even released in digital format in 2012 by the Federal Government. It is available at this free website: http://1940census.archives.gov/

Some census takers did not have exquisite handwriting and enlarging the print is a great tool when trying to decipher handwriting. The great thing about a digitized photograph is the ability to enlarge the print so try to obtain a digital copy of any census record sheet whenever possible.

Census records in the USA are available since 1790 but the census of 1890 is scant due to the records having been destroyed. Before 1790, tax lists were used in many localities. If you do not have a computer at home, you can go to many local libraries, State Archives or historical societies to access previous census records on microfilm.

Here are some tips concerning Census records.

➔ WORK BACKWARD - Start with the most recent

census available on an individual and work backward in time. It is tempting to go the other way when you inherit research records from others but you will quickly run into brick walls trying to fill the gap between you and a distant ancestor. You will make better and quicker progress working backward.

→ OBTAIN BLANK CENSUS FORMS - At the time each census was taken, different questions were asked of the individuals and their families. Blank census forms are useful when trying to figure out the information you can learn from each census. You can obtain free blank census forms at:

http://www.genealogy.com/00000023.html

→ BE AWARE OF TRANSCRIPTION MISTAKES – Many census records are now available for free on the internet but most of these are transcribed census records or indexes. Though census transcriptions are helpful in locating your ancestor, do not depend totally on transcribed census records to find your ancestor. Many transcriptions are inaccurate due to the poor handwriting on a census and each transcriber may decipher names differently.*

→ USE DIGITAL IMAGES WHENEVER POSSIBLE Digital images of census records are the best, since you will be able to actually view the original sheet of the census taker. Large commercial companies like Ancestry.com have digitized census records and you can have access to them for a yearly fee. Take advantage of Ancestry.com's free trial for fourteen days. Often, you just insert the name you are searching for in the search box and a list of possible matches will be provided. However, be wary, the name may still be transcribed wrong and you may think you have reached a brick wall when it was only a transcription error that created a problem for you. Sometimes you may have to look through individual census sheets to find your ancestor. Be tenacious in your search.

→ FREE SOURCES FOR CENSUS RECORDS – Though researching on your computer from home is convenient, it can become expensive because many commercial enterprises require a subscription fee to view their records. If you had rather not pay a fee, you can access census records recorded on Microfilm from all over the United States for free at many large libraries, State Archives or local LDS** Family History centers.

→ LIBRARY HELP - Many libraries have wonderful genealogy departments with very helpful librarians with genealogy research knowledge. Often, these libraries have classes for those interested in genealogy research. Some census records at the libraries are now being digitized as well and are much easier to read than the old microfilm. You can also access free digitized census records through a library that subscribes to ProQuest. Most libraries will let their patrons access the records for free and in many cases, you may have the option of logging onto HeritageQuest from the library or from home with your library card number. To find a local library with access to HeritageQuest, visit website: http://www.eogen.com/heritagequestonline   Another good website with links to free census records is http://www.census-online.com/links/  Some of the links to the records are transcribed records but some provide digitized images.

→ SOUNDEX SYSTEM - When you visit research census records, you must know the full name and the state or territory they possibly resided at the time the census was taken. Census takers recorded information under the head of the household. And the next thing you will be confronted with is the soundex system so a brief explanation of the soundex system may be helpful before venturing further. The soundex system is basically a coded last name index based on the way a surname sounds. Therefore last names (surnames) that sound the same may be spelled differently. To alleviate this problem, the soundex system was developed to find the surnames even when their maybe various spellings. Every code consists of a letter and three numbers such as W-252, the soundex code for Washington. The letter is the beginning letter of the surname and the numbers assigned according to a code. In the case of Washington as a surname the code means W, 2 for the S, 5 for the N, 2 for the G, with the remaining letters disregarded) If this sounds complicated, don't worry, there will generally be a librarian or other genealogists at the center to help you find the code for the surname you are seeking. If you want to know the soundex code before you venture to a research center, this website has a soundex calculator:

http://www.eogn.com/soundex

More detailed information on the soundex system can be found at the following website:

http://www.archives.gov/genealogy/census/soundex.h

tml.  When you find out the code, for a surname, write it down on the individual Group sheets.

→ USE ALTERNATIVE SPELLINGS - Remember to use alternative spellings of a surname. Many people could not read or write and census takers often wrote down what they assumed was the spelling of a name, usually this was a phonetic spelling. When pronouncing a surname, also, consider the dialect the individual may have used when giving his/her name to a census taker. The United States is a melting pot of many immigrants from other countries and often the newly arrived immigrants spoke little English. The census taker was again handicapped in trying to determine the spelling of names due to the various dialects he confronted and sometimes this was very different from the previous census taker's interpretation.*

→ MAKE A COPY - If you are lucky enough to find the family you are researching in a census, make a copy or if you find it on a computer, save it on your computer. Copies do not cost much and are usually free on the computer. You will be thankful that you saved the copy in the future when you need proof and the census sheet may provide other information you are not aware of immediately such as close neighbors who just might be related. Then as soon as possible, file the census sheet in your individual research file or attach it to the individual you are researching on your computer. You will not spend hours, retracing steps trying to find the census form again.

*This happened to me when I began my genealogy quest while researching the name Causey. The name Causey was spelled many ways over the years, such as Cawsey, Coosey, Casey, Kawsey and others and I had been unable to find the family in any 1920 census records. I knew the locality they were thought to have been residing at the time and decided I would have to look at each individual sheet to find them. After a long grueling day, with no success, I almost gave up but then toward the end of the next to the last page of microfilm, I found the family listed as Casey with the mother, father, and one child's names spelled correctly. I even found a lead for further research via an aunt and two cousins who were living with them at the time. I felt like shouting from the mountain tops but managed to hold my emotions in check until I was in my car.

**The Church of Jesus Christ of Latter-Day Saints have digitized genealogy records throughout the world. These centers are almost everywhere and are free to research.

## Tip Number Six
# REQUESTING
# COPIES of VITAL
# RECORDS

Vital records include Birth, Marriage, Divorce, Social Security, Military Records and Death records, all of which provide essential clues. However, in order to protect individual rights, there are laws to govern access to these records and with the rise in identity theft, increasingly, local governments take the guardianship of these records seriously, especially with more recent birth and death records.

Many states only open vital records, such as birth certificates to parties involved. States were required to maintain records since the 1800's but some states did not organize vital records until the early 1900's. The Center for Disease Control and Prevention maintains an up to date online source for all states and requirements governing the request; http://www.cdc.gov/nchs/w2w.htm If you are lucky enough to acquire vital records, a great deal of information can be derived from them.

→ BIRTH CERTIFICATES - From birth certificates you will often find the exact name of the individual. Sometimes people are given a nickname at birth, and were known only by the nickname throughout their lives, even in legal papers, because they didn't like their real names. Birth certificates also reveal the place of birth, exact date of birth and the names of the parents and even sometimes where the parents were born. All are vital clues in your family research. Though most information entered on provided on birth certificates can be considered accurate because it is usually filled out by the parents, some inaccuracies do occur.

→ MARRIAGE CERTIFICATES - Marriage certificates will provide the bride's and groom's full names, date of the marriage and the location where the marriage took place. Some include other information like the name and birthplace of their parents, the former residences of the bride and groom, names of witnesses and previous marriages.

→ DEATH CERTIFICATES - Death Certificates may be filled out during a difficult period by a grieving spouse or family member. The date and cause of death will probably be accurate but other information may be suspect so keep this in mind when reviewing the data provided.

→ SOCIAL SECURITY DEATH INDEX - Social Security Death Index is a great database that contains the names, dates of birth and death for over 77 million Americans and is a boon for genealogists. It is available online for free research at many locations. The following source at rootsweb even prints out a form letter to send for the record. http://ssdi.rootsweb.ancestry.com/ It also provides research for Railroad and Retirement Board Records.

→ MILITARY RECORDS - Military Records provide a great deal of information and often even include a description of the individual such as build, color of eyes, hair and any disabilities. Many copies of these records can be obtained through subscription memberships at the following websites:

http://www.footnote.com/?xid=319

http://www.ancestry.com/

If you know in specific information on your ancestor's military service, be sure to try a Google search. Many individual people are transcribing service information on particular military units especially on Civil War era service.

Another good source for all vital records is The National Archives at http://www.archives.gov/ Many records are accessible online and the National Archives website provides tutorial information on how to best utilize the website.

## Tip Number Seven
## COURT RECORDS
## RESEARCH

As you research expands, you will probably find a trip to courthouses beneficial. Original documents such as deeds, land grants, wills, guardianship or adoption records, tax records, information on the community and other resources are often found in Courthouses and are only scantily available online. They are considered public domain material and can be accessed and searched by any citizen.

Below are some tips to remember in planning your visit.

→ VERIFY COURTHOUSE - First, make sure you are doing research in the right courthouse. County (or Parish, Shire) geographical and political lines were often changed by government or political intervention. Your ancestor may have remained at one residence but found their residence was in a different government jurisdiction at various time periods. Sometimes, you might discover that an ancestor's resided in one county but some or even all of his/her records could be found in the adjoining county. This would be especially true if they lived in a county line or they owned a large amount of land in more than one county. Historical societies, State Archives and libraries are good resources to discover geographical and political histories of your ancestors.

→ CHECK WITH COURTHOUSE IN ADVANCE - Contact the courthouse in advance of your visit to find out about any access restrictions, closed dates and hours available for your research. You do not want to travel across the country only to find out the courthouse is closed on the day of your visit or that records are not accessible. Also, ask if copying equipment is available and if there is anyone available to help with your research. Sometimes a librarian, local historical society or even just a local citizen will be willing to assist you. Have a goal in mind to make the most of your trip. Make a list of specific names, dates and details for each individual ancestor and focus your research on these documenting the components.

→ STORAGE PROBLEMS - Many local courthouses do not have the time to adequately store old records so don't be surprised at what you discover. There may be little if any organization and limited space so don't plan to take many belongings with you. Notepads, pencils, and change for copying should always be packed. Take a digital camera if it is allowed. A good digital camera often makes great copies of wills, deeds, etc. and you have the added advantage of enlarging the picture on a computer. You need a steady hand for documents. Be sure to have a charged battery if you have a laptop computer but make sure they are allowed before bringing one. There are usually various offices in a courthouse but a directory to the offices should be near the front door and will help you find where the documents are kept.

→ PLAN YOUR TRIP - After reaching the courthouse location, you may soon realize that it would take many hours to research all the records of your ancestors on one trip so plan your trip in advance. Take a deep breath, and focus on the goal you made for the trip. Indexes are usually kept on deeds, wills, and most court records. They are the first choice for helping you to locate records.

→ COURTHOUSE STAFF - Staff at archives, courthouses or libraries are usually helpful but remember they have a job to do so respect their time and avoid asking them specific questions not related to your research. Never waste their time with a "rambling family story." They do not have the time to listen. When you need to approach a staff member, ask specific questions, such as: "Could I see the deed (will, court minutes) indexes for the years 1850 to 1870?" They will probably take you to a vault or sometimes just point you in the direction of the indexes. Remember, clerks are not genealogists so do not ask the clerks about genealogy "how to" questions.

→ OTHER RESEARCHERS - Ofter researchers such as title searchers, local land companies, attorneys and other genealogists may be working in the area as well so do not take up too much of the often valuable counter space for your materials. If you have trouble understanding an Index, ask the clerk to explain it to you if he/she is available. Other experienced researchers are often very good resources for answers to specific questions but never ask too many questions. After all, he/she probably has limited time at the courthouse as well.

→ MAKE DIGITAL COPIES - Make good photocopies or digital photos of everything that is allowed. You will have time to examine the document photograph more at home. With today's computer software, you can even enlarge the picture. If you are not allowed to copy a document, write down a transcription (with misspelling) or at least notes of the document if you are pressed for time but be sure to add the complete source for each document. Look for indexes of deeds, wills, and other court documents with the surname you are researching and make a copy. They could be related family members. You may be able to request a copy of a document when you return home when you have specific index information. Never request copies just before closing time and be prepared for a high fees. Often, it is $1 a page or more.

→ SEARCH FOR ORIGINAL RECORDS - Look for original records that have not be microfilmed or digitized. Records that have been digitized or microfilmed can usually be obtained online. Even if there is a fee to acquire the document online, it will certainly be less expensive than a trip across the country to a small courthouse.

→ LOCAL RESEARCHERS - Perhaps your short visit is over and you still have so much more research to be done in the courthouse you visited. Before leaving, check to see if their is someone locally you could hire to do research for you. Often, there is someone in the community who loves history and will, for a small fee, provide the time needed to adequately search the courthouse. He/She is probably also well-acquainted and on very good terms with the local staff and will be a tremendous help in future genealogical researches in the area. Above all, be courteous and friendly to the staff and thank them for their assistance.

→ BURNED COURTHOUSES - Sometimes, old courthouses burned or records were lost beyond repair but don't give up. The records may have been moved to the State at an early date or possibly be found in the State archives. Other resources include LDS Family History Centers and where you might discover Court records that were digitized or microfilmed before they were lost.

# Tip Number Eight
# CHURCH RECORDS
# AND
# NEWSPAPER RESEARCH

Other great sources of information include Church Records, Newspapers. In Church records you will often find Membership , Birth, Marriage, Baptism, Death, Confirmation, Communion, Church School, Church Cemetery and Burial Records as well as Church Board or Society Minutes. When you discover your ancestor's religion, study, the history of his/her religion. Many times valuable insights as to the reason for their migration to another locality. Also, by studying the history of a specific religion, you will discover where the records were stored, sometimes they may be in obscure locations.

→ CHURCH RECORDS - The first place to look for Church Records is of course, the church where your ancestor was a member, if it still exists. If the original Church no longer exists, check to see if it was merged with another church. Sometimes you may find that husbands and wives belonged to different churches at the same time. Ask questions of ministers, elderly people or others in the area. You may discover quite a bit of history. The history of many small towns is now being recorded online and sometimes information about local churches is included. Check Genealogical and historical periodicals

33

of the area. Many old church records have been published by historical societies. Some are even in book form and can be found in local large libraries with other genealogy information. Many Church Records have been microfilmed and can be found online in local county genealogy sites.

→ NEWSPAPERS - Old newspapers can often be found on Microfilm in State Archives, local libraries, newspaper office archives, colleges, historical societies and online. The United States Newspaper Program, USNP is a cooperative national effort among the states and the federal government to locate, catalog and preserve on microfilm newspapers published in the eighteenth century to the present website: http://www.neh.gov/projects/usnp.html

→ MICROFILMED RECORDS - The Microfilmed copies of newspapers are available to researchers on interlibrary loan. Newspapers provide, obituaries, births, deaths, social events, court records, political events, illnesses, visitors to a community, state wide news, school news and often mentions local names. They are a wonderful resource for researching genealogy.

# Tip Number Nine
## SOME TIPS TO
## BREAK
## THAT BRICK WALL

Anyone interested in genealogy has at one time or other hit the proverbial brick wall on a family tree line, when no lead develops and your ancestor just seems to disappear. It can become very frustrating.

Here are some suggestions for breaking down that wall:

→ RETRACE YOUR STEPS - Create a time-line, Record every event that you have found about the person.

→ LOOK FOR TIME-LINE GAPS - Are there any long gaps when the person could not be found? If so, focus on the last known location and study the geography, history or any collateral records related to the event in which the person was involved. There may be a clue in records of fellow relatives or friends involved in the event.

→ CHECK OTHER FAMILY MEMBERS – Remember to check newspapers, military records, land records, wills, and obituaries of other family members around the "time gap" for clues. You might find the person mentioned in another family member's deed, will, or obituary with a location.

→ TRY OTHER NAME SPELLINGS - Get creative with

the spelling of the surname when searching the records. Try unusual phonetic spellings. Many dialects often played havoc with census takers. They often, did not hear the name pronounced correctly or left off endings. Wild guesses of the spelling of names were often made.

→ NEW LOCATIONS - While looking at your time-line, follow the locations. This includes collateral family members or friends. Groups of people often move together to new locations.

→ CHECK FOR TRAVEL - Check ship passenger lists. Your ancestor may have traveled to another country. Check Military records, Church records, Newspaper articles and notices, school records, official certificates around the time your ancestor was missing for clues.

→ COURT RECORDS - Check deeds, grants, mortgages and other land records. They sometimes mention the location of family members. Probate and estate records often mention the residence of related parties. Court records of you ancestor's last known location may mention your your relative.

→ CHALLENGE WHAT YOU KNOWN - Was this information a family story? Could there be an invalid assumption in your data? Many false assumptions are made with census records. If children are living in a house with two adults, it is logical to assume that this is one family with their children. However, many times this is not the case. It was common practice for children to be apprenticed to other families when their own parents died or sometimes they were just visiting but included in the census.

→ GRANDPARENTS – In times past, Grandparents "took in" grandchildren and raised them as their own. People married again quite soon after the death of a spouse and brought the children of a former marriage with them. Reevaluate your documentation. Are you sure all the children belonged to the parents listed?

→ TRADITIONAL STORIES - Stories 'handed down' in the family are known for having problems and the invalid information often continues through many generation to the point that it almost become a fact. Verify all your family stories.

→ CHECK ASSUMPTIONS - Do you have too many assumptions in your data? Write down everything you know about the person who disappeared. Then verify all the information with proof.

## Tip Number Ten
# GENEALOGY MYTHS
## and
# DOCUMENTATION

Good genealogy research takes time. There is just no way around it. I wish it was possible that with a few clicks on your computer keyboard, you could find your family ancestry but that is not the case. There are many myths floating around out there in the world of genealogy, making it harder for genealogists and if you do much research, you'll run across them.

Don't derail your research by becoming a victim to the following false myths.

→ FAMILY HISTORY ONLINE - It looks so simple on in Advertisements and on the TV show *Who do you think you are?* A few clicks on the keyboard and you find your family history but genealogy research is a lot more complicated than that. You can obtain lots of actual records online but there are also many errors in these records, including family trees. To adequately document your family tree, you need actual documents that often requires visits to Libraries, Courthouses and Archives. In your research, you will run across other genealogy books and published records by other researchers but publishing research does not make it accurate. Even professional genealogists make mistakes. Invalid assumptions can be made, transcription errors occur and your family member may have been mistaken about family history. The internet is in some ways compounds mistakes because errors made in works in the past are being repeated again though digitizing and transcribing these original errors. The repetition of an error does not make it correct. All facts must be verified and documented.

→ WATCH FOR FRAUDULENT GENEALOGIES – Around the In the 19th and 20th century, many family genealogies were produced to prove descent from founding fathers and genealogy. Since genealogy was a source of income, sometimes if a black sheep was discovered, a genealogy history may have been improved on and information dropped concerning the errant ancestor. Many fraudulent pedigrees were done during this time.

→ COURTHOUSE BURNED, ALL RECORDS ARE GONE - You may run into a courthouse fire. (and this is a good argument of why we need to digitize all court records but that's another story). If you run into this situation, remember, many vital records, naturalizations, deeds, wills and other records weren't always completely destroyed. Sometimes records survived or copies were sent to another office or agency.

→ 1890 CENSUS BURNED - It is true that more than 99 per cent was burned in a fire at the Commerce Building on Jan 10, 1921. However, when the fire broke out firefighters flooded the basement with water and the flames didn't spread to upper floors. The 1890 records were piled outside a records storage vault and were soaked. They set in storage for a while and sometime between 1933 and 1935, the records were destroyed. Fragments of the 1890 census with 6,160 names from the states of Illinois, Ohio, Alabama, Georgia and North Carolina later turned up and are available on microfilm.

→ THREE BROTHERS STORY – The story goes: '*There were three brothers who came to America.*' One went north, one went south and the third went west. Oftentimes, this is an excuse for lazy genealogists who cannot explain why the same surname exists in different places. Many times, the families were not related at all. This story is now so common that if you hear it......consider it a red flag that other data may be false or not well researched.

→ NAME CHANGE AT ELLIS ISLAND - Your may hear that your ancestor's name was changed at Ellis Island. Passenger lists were created at the port of departure and Ellis Island officially checked the names on the list. However, immigrants often changed their own names in an attempt to sound more American. Sometimes they changed their names because of a family event in an attempt to become anonymous.

→ FAMOUS ANCESTOR - I hate to be the bearer of bad news but many times in your ancestry research you will discover that the oral tradition "handed" down in your family stating that your ancestry includes Mayflower descendants, royalty, or other famous people may not be true. Often, family trees were inadvertently embellished in the past by some well meaning person and this 'oral tradition' continued down through the generations. Lots of families have these stories and they became embellished over time, so be sure to do your research to validate. Not everyone with the same last name is related. DNA evidence today has disproved many long held traditional family stories about descendants. So beware, as you seek documentation on your information, someone in your family may become upset it you debunk an 'oral tradition'.

→ FAMILY CREST ONLINE - Actually, families don't have crests, individuals do. Coats of arms must be granted and you must prove descent through a male line of someone to whom arms were granted. Be cautious with advertisements of books with your family surname in America. Usually they advertise a coat of arms and surname books and are quite expensive. These are generic family histories and are not **your** specific family history. The list of names included are probably taken from the phone book.

→ WITCHES BURNED – You may hear the story of a gr-gr- grandmother being burned at the stake as a witch in Salem, Massachusetts. Witches were never burned at the stake in North America. All the witches were hanged except for Giles Cory who was pressed to death.

→ TOWN NAMED AFTER MY FAMILY IN ENGLAND OR EUROPE - The truth is that towns were generally started before people had surnames so it is probably the other way around. Your family adopted the name of the town. But this still gives you a good clue as to the home of your ancestral family.

→ DESCENDED FROM CHEROKEE PRINCESS – *'Our family descends from a Cherokee princess.'* Royalty titles were not used in North American Indians. This rumor started when Pocahontas arrived in England. The newspapers claimed she was a princess to create publicity.

→ DESCENDANT OF ROBERT E. LEE - Actually, there were thousands of Lee's in the mid-1800's and most were not related to each other. Lee was a very common name and this makes it difficult to research but this legend is more than likely a result of wishful thinking by those who lived in the South.

→ MAYFLOWER ANCESTOR - *'My ancestor arrived on the Mayflower.'* This one is also usually a result of wishful thinking. Luckily William Bradford recorded all 102 passengers on the Mayflower in 1650 and about half died the first year. To prove this claim, you must be able to document descent from one of the surviving passengers listed at the website below:
http://www.rootsweb.com/~mosmd/mayfpas.htm

→ ROYALTY ANCESTORS - *'Our family descends from Royalty.'* Believe it or not, this may have a ring of truth. If you go back thousands of years in your ancestry, you will have billions of ancestors and the odds are that a few of these billions of ancestors were members of royal families or had money. But you must document your descent from one of them. That is the fun part of genealogy!

If you discover a story is false, don't throw it out completely. There's still a possibility of a kernel of truth in the story and it was simply enriched with each telling as it was handed down in the family.

It is never easy to debunk a family story and if you

are the person who discovers the truth, beware....there may be some resentment from family members. Long held family stories are hard to "let go of" but in the interest of accuracy, we must do as one Alabama Pioneer member emailed when she encountered resentment, "Just do your research and let the chips fall where they may." Future generations will be thankful for your effort.

# FINAL THOUGHTS AND TIPS
## ON GENEALOGY
### RESEARCH

Genealogy is becoming one of the fastest growing hobbies in the United States. The FamilySearch Web site of the LDS family history library has six to seven million hits a day. Researching your family roots provides a connection with your ancestors and helps you understand more about yourself but to get the most out of your research, it is important to remember the following tips.

→ DOCUMENTATION - **Always** document your sources and if possible make a copy of the original document. Granted, research by others is always helpful and saves you considerable time but always remember to follow up and document the research with actual supporting records. This will add credibility to your research and help future researchers of your family surname. It need not be expensive. Often this data can be obtained free online and many courthouses, archives and libraries provide copies of documents for a small fee. Future family researchers will appreciate your effort to document.

→ LIFE STORIES - Be sure to write down life stories. Genealogy is more than just names and "who was related to who." Collect the stories and you will enjoy it more. Interview your elderly relatives and record their stories before they are forgotten forever.

→ HAVE FUN! - Most of all, have fun! You will soon discover that genealogy is like a gigantic puzzle that never has an end. Each clue or piece of information leads to many more questions. You will become close to your ancestor's and really admire their fortitude and the courage it took to create their life.

If you stick with your research, one day you will hold in your hand a document your ancestor's held one hundred years ago, or stand on land where he settled. In that moment, you will feel a connection with your ancestor and sense of purpose in your life that is hard to describe. Your will never look at your life the same way again. In that moment, you too, "caught the genealogy bug."

# APPENDIX
## SOME
## INTERVIEW QUESTIONS
## TO ASK ELDERLY RELATIVES

1)What is your full name and why were you given this name?
2)When and where were you born?
3)What was happening in the world when you were born?
4)What was your mother's full maiden name, birth date and place of birth?
5)Do you remember a special story your mother told about growing up?
6)What was a precious memory you had about your mother?
7)What were your brother's and sister's full name?
8)What are some things you use to do together?
9)What do you do together now?
10)How often do you see your family members?
11)What is your earliest memory of home?
12)Did you have a favorite hiding place as a child?
13)As a child, what did you love to play?
14)Where did you live as a child?
15)Where did you play with your friends?
16)What was your favorite store and why did you like to go there?
17)Where did you worship when you were growing up?
18)Where did your father work?
19)What did your mother do during the day...did she work?
20)What chores were you responsible for?

21)What did you like to do during the summer/fall/winter/spring?

22)Did you have a favorite book/game/treat/poem/toy?

23)Did you have a pet....what was its name?

24)What kind of car did your family drive?

25)How did people dress?

26)What is something you always wanted?

27)How were girls/boys expected to behave when you were growing up?

28)What was the most wonderful thing about your father/mother?

29)What was your father/mother especially good at doing?

30)What were some lessons you learned from your father/mother?

31)What was your father/mother's best piece of advice?

32)Did your mother have a favorite recipe?

33)What elementary school/high school/ college did you attend?

34)Did you have a favorite teacher, if so, why was he/she your favorite?

35)What was your best subject?

36)Did you have a special school event that was especially memorable?

37)Who were some of your friends?

38)What were some popular fads when you were in school?

39)What were some of your favorite songs and musicians?

40)What kind of music do you enjoy now?

41)What was the most important thing you learned in school?

42)Did you have a favorite hymn or song?

43) Tell me about the first time you drove a car?

44)When were you allowed to date/ wear lipstick?

45)Who was your best childhood friend?

46)What have you learned about getting along with others?

47)What was your first real job?

48)Who was your first "crush", boyfriend/girlfriend?

49)Do you have any special memories about dating, first kiss, broken heart, etc.?

50)What is an important lesson you hope all your children and grandchildren learn?

51)When did you first vote in an election?

52)What was your best family vacation?

53)What place would you most like to see?

54)What was a goal you set and reached?

55)How old were you and what where you doing when you met your husband/wife?

56)When and how did he propose?

57)What was the day, time and place you were married...what did you wear...did you have attendants or honeymoon?

58)Where did you first live?

59)What is something you and your spouse still laugh about?

60)Name your children, and birth dates.

61)Where did you worship?

62)What did you love most about being a mother/father and what was the most difficult thing about being a mother/father?

63)Do you have a special Scripture?

64) Tell me about a memorable Christmas?

65)What did you do every Christmas...any special traditions?

66)What was a favorite Christmas recipe you enjoyed?

67)What are some of your favorite authors, books?

68)Do you have a cherished piece of jewelry...why do you cherish it?

69)What do you value most in life?

70)What is your most comforting possession?
71)What is your favorite hobby?
72)Who do miss seeing the most?
73)What does real success mean to you?
74)What is the most important thing in life to you?
75)What do you want to do in your twenties?
76)What did you do in your thirties, forties?
77)What did you discover in your fifties?
78)What do you consider failure?
79)Where did you live in your twenties/
thirties/forties/fifties?
80)What is your current address?
81)Is there something you would especially like to do?

# GENEALOGY WEBSITES
## for
## BEGINNERS

•Ancestry.com - http://www.ancestry.com subscription fee - (sometimes has limited free trial)

•Cindi's List - http://www.cyndislist.com/ Links to Genealogy sites worldwide -Free

•GenForum - http://genforum.genealogy.com/ surname queries  -Free

•FootNote.com - http://www.footnote.com/ -Many documents -subscription fee

•RootsWeb.com - http://www.footnote.com/ -Mostly free

•USGenWeb.org - http://usgenweb.org/ -Free, Volunteers submit information

•Interment.net - http://www.interment.net/ -Free, Online cemetery records

•findagrave.com - http://www.findagrave.com/ -Free, volunteers submit, registration

•Genealogy.com - http://www.genealogy.com/ -Membership fee

•HeritageQuest - http://www.eogen.com/heritagequestonline – Free through library

•Census-online - http://www.census-online.com/ -Links to online census records

•USGenNet - http://www.usgennet.org/ -Free records

•WorldGenWeb - http://www.worldgenweb.org/ -Free -non profit -volunteers

•FamilySearch.org - http://www.familysearch.org/-Free - family search

•Familytreemagazine.comhttp://www.familytreemagazine.com /freeforms/ -Free forms

15884102R00036

Made in the USA
Charleston, SC
25 November 2012